Contents

Taste this

You have five senses that give you all kinds of information about what is going on around you.

Your five senses are sight, touch, taste, smell and hearing. This book is about taste.

Your sense of taste tells you about the food you eat and drink.

Let's Start!
Science

Tastes good!

Sally Hewitt

QED Publishing

First published in the UK in 2005 by
QED Publishing
A Quarto Group company
226 City Road
London EC1V 2TT

www.qed-publishing.co.uk

A Catalogue record for this book is
available from the British Library.

ISBN 1 84538 446 6

Written by Sally Hewitt

Project Editor: Honor Head
Series Designer: Zeta Jones
Photographer: Michael Wicks
Picture Researcher: Nic Dean
Series Consultant: Sally Morgan

Publisher: Steve Evans
Creative Director: Louise Morley
Editorial Manager: Jean Coppendale

Printed and bound in China

Picture credits

Key: t = top, b = bottom, m = middle,
l = left, r = right

Corbis/Wartenberg/Picture Press 4,
/Richard Hutchings 8b, /Owen Franken 9t,
/Lynda Richardson 9b;

Getty Images/PBJ Pictures/Stone 6, 20b,
/Phil Boorman/Taxi 8r, /Ryan McVay/Taxi
12, /Xavier Bonghi/The Image Bank 14,
/Melanie Acevedo/Foodpix 20t.

The author and publisher would like to
thank Sam, Georgina, Millie, Emily and
Lakia.

The words in **bold**
are explained in the
Glossary on page 22.

Everything you eat has its own taste.
You remember what food tastes like
if you have eaten it before.

Have you tasted any
of these foods?

lemon

Can you say what
they taste like?

apples

pepper

carrot

Your taste

You usually choose food because you like the taste of it.

What is your favourite food?

What is your least favourite food?

◀ Do you like trying food you have never eaten before?

Not everyone likes the same tastes.

Ask your family and friends which of these foods they like.

Tick each box like this:

	Love	Like	Don't like
Broccoli		✔✔	
Chocolate	✔✔✔		
Strawberry	✔	✔	✔
Spicy curry	✔	✔✔	✔

Count the ticks. Which is the most popular food? What does it taste like?

Stick out your tongue

Your tongue is the part of your body you taste with. It is covered in tiny **taste buds**.

Different parts of your tongue taste different flavours.

Does my ice-cream taste **salty**, **sour**, **bitter** or **sweet**?

bitter

sweet and salty

sour

8

When you eat food, your tongue tells your brain what you are tasting.

When food tastes sweet, such as honey, you may want to eat more.

▲ If food tastes bitter, you want to spit it out.

Find the flavour

Some food doesn't taste very strong. It doesn't have much flavour.

You can add flavours, such as salt and pepper, to make food taste better.

This needs pepper.

Some flavours taste delicious together, others taste strange.

Activity

Try this test to see which flavours make food taste better or worse.

Add a little bit of each of these flavours – salt, jam, lemon juice and tomato sauce – to pieces of chocolate, apple, carrot and bread.

Which flavours do you think taste good together.

Taste and smell

Smell and taste work together to help you enjoy your food. A delicious smell tells your brain that the food will taste good!

When you have a cold and can't smell very well, your food doesn't taste as strong as usual.

This smells good.

You use your senses of smell and sight, as well as your sense of taste, to tell you what you are eating.

Ask a friend to shut his or her eyes and hold their nose while they eat pieces of...

orange

radish

doughnut

cheese

Can your friend tell you what the food is just by the taste? Does smelling the food make it taste stronger?

Chew and swallow

When you are about to eat your favourite food, does your mouth water? The water in your mouth is called **saliva**.

Sometimes the smell of food by itself makes your mouth water.

Saliva makes your food easier to swallow.

◀ When you eat, the saliva in your mouth covers your food as you chew it.

Saliva carries the taste of your food into your taste buds.

Not so tasty now.

Does chewing gum stay tasty as you keep chewing?

▲ Chew a piece of bread for a long time. Does the taste change?

Do you have to chew a lollipop to taste it?

Fresh and tasty

Fresh food looks
and smells
delicious.
You want
to eat it!

A date on
packets of
food helps
you to know
it is fresh.

After that date, the food starts to go bad
or **stale** and will not taste so good.

Old and stale food
doesn't look good.
It smells horrid.
It will taste horrid.

You don't want
to eat it!

The look, smell and
taste warn you,
this food
isn't fresh!

▶ Old food can
make you ill. You
should always
throw it away.

Tasty colours

The colour of food can help us to know what it will taste like.

strawberry

How many blue foods can you think of? What do they taste like?

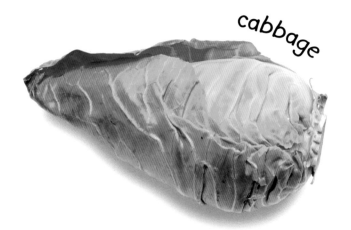
banana

Orange food might taste of carrots or oranges, but not cabbage!

cabbage

Would you like to eat this food?

Strange-coloured food makes you think it will taste strange, too!

Draw food you like to eat. Give it colours and patterns, like the food in the picture.

Ask your friends what it might taste like.

Would they like to eat it?

New tastes

At the shops, you can buy different food from around the world.

▲ Chillies and spices make curry hot and tasty.

There are all kinds of flavours you may not have tasted before. Try them. You might like them!

You can add new foods and flavours to soup and fruit salad.

Activity

Try something new. Put a different vegetable in your vegetable soup and add a pinch of herbs.

Chop a new fruit into your fruit salad and add a drop of vanilla.

What new food or flavour could you add to your pizza or sandwich?

Glossary

Bitter
Coffee often tastes bitter.

Fresh
Fresh food is new. It is just right to eat.

Saliva
Saliva is the spit in your mouth. It helps you to taste and swallow food.

Salty
When food tastes of salt, it is salty.

Sour
Lemon tastes sour.

Stale
Stale food is old. It is starting to dry out and smell.

Sweet
Sugar tastes sweet.

Taste buds
Tiny bumps on your tongue which tell you if your food tastes sweet, sour, salty or bitter.

Index

Parents' and teachers' notes

TEACHER SAFETY NOTE:
If you are having a tasting at school, ask each child to bring a letter from home telling you of any food allergies or confirming the child has none.

- Encourage children to predict the taste of foods. Will the apple taste sweet or sour? How will lemon juice make apple taste? Will I like the taste of apple and lemon juice together?

- Find words about taste throughout the book, such as flavour, sweet, sour, bitter and salty. Talk about how different foods taste using these words. Write poems or stories using these words.

- Create your own Taste Tables. Collect drawings and photographs of food for each of the taste groups – sweet, sour, salty and bitter. Stick the pictures onto four large sheets of paper. Are there any similarities between the foods? For example, are all the sweet foods fruit?

- Talk about food hygiene and safety. Never taste unfamiliar food, berries or nuts without first checking with an adult. Always wash your hands before handling food. Make sure food is clean, fresh or well-cooked before tasting it.

- Divide the class into groups. Ask them to put together a montage of their favourite meal using cut-out pictures or their own drawings. They must have at least one food from each of the taste groups, for example, a flavouring, such as lemon for sour. Ask them to label all the foods they have chosen with one of the taste groups.

- When you go to the market, talk about the food you buy. Discuss the tastes you like and don't like. Choose an unfamiliar food and talk about what it might taste like. Prepare and eat it together. Use this as an opportunity to discover new foods for the whole family to try.

- Sort fruit and vegetables into colours. Discuss whether all yellow food tastes the same. Taste banana, yellow pepper and lemon and talk about the different flavours. Which taste group do they each belong to?